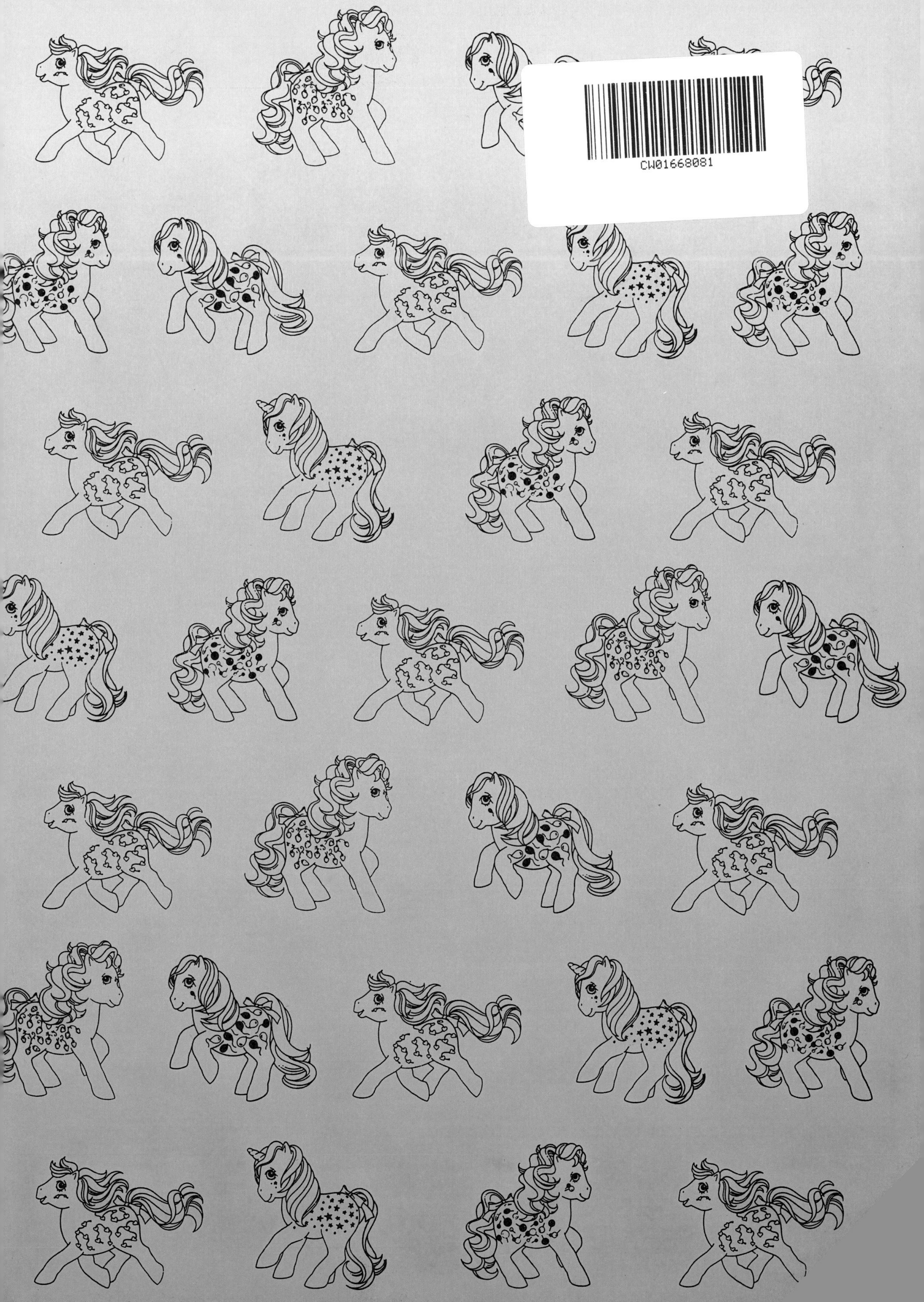

My Little Pony

ANNUAL 1989

Contents

Lollipop and the Nonsense Gnome 5
Love Melody's Song Book I 14
Journey on the Magic Balloon 15
The Enchanted Table 22
Tea Party in Funfair Forest 30
Love Melody's Song Book II 32
Milky Way and the Whispering Whirlpool 33
The Mitten Tree 40
The Runaway Toothpaste 49
Midnight Magic 56
A Race to the Hair Salon 62

Published in Great Britain by
World International Publishing Limited,
An Egmont Company,
Egmont House, P.O. Box 111, Great Ducie Street,
Manchester M60 3BL.
Printed in Italy.
ISBN 7235 6829 4

Stories by Pat Posner

LOLLIPOP AND THE NONSENSE GNOME

It was a lovely sunny day and Lollipop felt very happy as she hurried to the walled garden where her magic lollipop tree grew. "Muddled manes, I've forgotten my key again," she laughed. "It's a good job I keep a spare one hidden under Signy's toe."

Signy was a pretty stone statue who guarded the door to the garden. She was one of Lollipop's special friends and only Lollipop knew that Signy could walk and talk. "Hello, Signy," chuckled Lollipop. "Please lift up your toe, I've forgotten my key again."

"I expect you were too busy thinking about your new juggling act," said Signy, as she daintily lifted her toe. "How many lollipops are you going to juggle with at the Green Gnome's party?"

"Twenty big ones and four little ones," replied Lollipop. "You see, Signy, twenty-four gnomes have passed all their tests and the Green Gnome is awarding them all with a magic spell book. He has asked the Party Ponies to use twenty-four of everything in their acts."

"Now I understand why I heard Love Melody singing so many songs last night," laughed Signy. "She must have been making up a song for each of the twenty-four gnomes. Strawberry Fair will have to shake her mane and make twenty-four dishes of sunny strawberries. Milky Way will make a shimmering arch with twenty-four stars. Up, Up and Away will wiggle her nose and make twenty-four balloons and Dancing Butterflies will dance with twenty-four magic butterflies!"

"That's right," agreed Lollipop. "And I'd better go and practise my juggling. I'll leave the door open then you can watch me."

So Lollipop unlocked the garden door and hurried over to her magic lollipop tree. "I'd like twenty big lollipops and four little ones, please," Lollipop told the tree.

At once, twenty-four lollipops jumped off the tree and twenty-four new ones began to grow. Lollipop's magic tree never ran out of lollipops! The only reason she kept the door to the garden locked was to stop the baby ponies having competitions to see who could pick and eat the most lollipops. Baby Bouncy had once made herself very ill doing that and hadn't been able to bounce around for days.

Before long, the little party pony was trotting around the garden juggling twenty-four lollipops. As Signy watched from the door, she joined in with Lollipop's juggling song.

"I'm a Party Pony, a juggler am I.
I'll juggle my lollipops into the sky!"

Lollipop sighed as one of the lollipops fell to the ground. "Oh, Signy, it's very hard to juggle twenty-four lollipops," she said. Signy didn't answer and Lollipop glanced round the garden. She knew somebody must be there if Signy wasn't talking. Somebody was there!

A little gnome, wearing green

boots, a red cloak and carrying an umbrella, laughed loudly and ran up to Lollipop. "You should be juggling with twenty-three lollipops," he laughed. "I also passed my tests, the Green Gnome will be awarding me with a magic spell book, too. Oh dear, oh dear, I'm so unhappy."

Lollipop stared in amazement as the little gnome laughed louder and louder. "Don't you mean I should be juggling with twenty-*five* lollipops?" she asked, feeling puzzled. "And why are you laughing if you're unhappy?"

"Don't you laugh when you're unhappy?" retorted the gnome. "And why aren't you wearing a raincoat? The sun is very hot today, you'll get soaking wet. Would you like to share my umbrella? I can make it bigger you know." The gnome muttered some words and the umbrella went smaller and smaller!

"There," he said. "Now there's room for both of us to keep wet underneath it. You will tell the Green Gnome to award me with a magic spell book, won't you? He does need one extra, so he'll have to have twenty-three books."

"Twenty-four plus one is twenty-five," laughed Lollipop.

"Oh dear, oh dear! Please don't cry, I didn't mean to upset you. Here, have a handkerchief," said the little gnome. He muttered some words and all at once it started to rain and the tiny umbrella disappeared.

"You've cried so many tears you've made the sun come out," he said crossly to Lollipop. "I'll have to take my boots off, they mustn't get wet."

Lollipop laughed even more as

the little gnome started to take his boots off. Instead of taking them off his feet, he pulled them up his legs then over his body until he disappeared inside them. "Open the door for me," he said in a muffled voice.

Lollipop looked at the boots and saw a little handle on the sole of one. She moved it downwards and the gnome yelled loudly from inside the boots. "I said open the door . . . not close the door." The little pony moved the handle upwards and the gnome popped out.

"I'm full up now, that was hard work," he said to Lollipop. "Have you got anything to eat? The sun has gone in again, but I can't be bothered to put my boots on."

The raindrops had disappeared and the sun was shining brightly. Lollipop tried not to laugh as she answered the gnome. She didn't want him to think she was crying again. "You can pick some lollipops from my tree," she said, wondering what would happen.

"I don't like lollipops," said the gnome and he started to cry. But Lollipop was beginning to understand the strange gnome. She knew he meant he *did* like lollipops and really he was laughing.

"You pick and eat as many as you like," she told him. "I'm going to practise my juggling. The party is this afternoon, I must make sure I'll be able to juggle properly."

Lollipop forgot all about the gnome for a while. Her juggling act was working well and she juggled faster and faster. Suddenly, some

balloons appeared and the little pony juggled with them, too.

"Well done!" praised Up, Up and Away, trotting over to join Lollipop. "That's the best juggling I've ever seen. And the lollipop-stick houses are the best I've ever seen as well. Who built them? They weren't here yesterday."

Lollipop looked round her garden. There were dozens of houses made from lollipop-sticks. Big houses, small houses, long houses . . .

"I knocked them down, aren't they horrible?" sobbed the gnome.

"Who's that?" asked Up, Up and Away. "What is he talking about?"

"He's a little gnome who gets everything mixed up," explained Lollipop. "He's . . . he's a nonsense gnome, that's what he is! He must have picked and eaten lots of lollipops then used the sticks to build these houses."

"I don't think he's a nonsense gnome;" said Up, Up and Away. "These houses are beautiful, I just wish I was small enough to go inside one and look around," she whispered.

"Don't say that, if the gnome hears you he'll try to make a spell," said Lollipop in alarm. "Then you'll either grow enormous or disappear."

"Who's disappearing?" asked the gnome coming nearer. "I can't see anyone. Where are they?"

"I see what you mean, he is all mixed up," smiled Up, Up and Away. "He was laughing because his houses were nice, not crying because they were horrible."

"That's wrong," said the gnome nodding his head. "I felt very sad when I'd knocked those horrible houses down. Shall I knock one down for you?" he added. "A tiny one you can go outside?"

"Shall I say yes or no?" whispered Up, Up and Away to Lollipop. "I would like him to build me one."

"Say yes," replied Lollipop. "He doesn't seem to mix up what we say, just what he says himself."

"Don't you want me to knock one down for you?" asked the gnome impatiently.

"Yes please," replied Up, Up and Away. "Oh, look," she added. "Here's Love Melody, I expect she wants us to listen to her twenty-four songs."

"Don't sing while I'm knocking this house down," said the gnome.

"It's all right," explained Lollipop. "He wants you to sing, Love Melody. When you've sung all your party songs maybe you could make up a song especially for the nonsense gnome."

So while the gnome built a lollipop-stick house for Up, Up and Away, Love Melody sang her pretty songs and Lollipop juggled her lollipops.

"Don't eat some lollipops, balloon pony," said the gnome. "I don't need some more sticks to knock your house down. I'm very hungry, I can eat lots more."

"Don't laugh, he'll think you're unhappy," Lollipop warned her friends. "Just eat some lollipops, Up, Up and Away. Then give the sticks to the nonsense gnome."

"Right," said the gnome after a while. "I've knocked it down. Isn't it tiny?" The new lollipop-stick house was perfect and just the right size for a little pony. Up, Up and Away trotted inside. The gnome had even made furniture for all the rooms!

"There's room for you inside," the gnome sobbed to Lollipop and Love Melody. Lollipop realized just in time that there was *not* room for more than one little pony *inside* the house!

"It's a shame he's such a nonsense gnome," said Lollipop. "The Green Gnome will never agree to give him a magic spell book."

"I don't want to go to the party. I don't, I don't!" laughed the gnome.

"That's his way of crying!" sighed Lollipop. "He'd love to go to the party."

"Well, we're the Party Ponies aren't we!" said Love Melody. "When we've performed our party acts at the party for the twenty-four clever gnomes, we'll come back here and have a special party for the nonsense gnome."

"That's a good idea," agreed Up, Up and Away, as she hurried out of the lollipop-stick house.

The Green Gnome's party was a great success. Lollipop juggled her lollipops; twenty big ones and four little ones. Love Melody sang twenty-four songs and when she took her final bow, twenty-four pink paper love hearts floated down to the gnomes who'd passed all their tests. Up, Up and Away wiggled her nose and made twenty-four balloons while Dancing Butterflies danced in the sky with her magic butterflies.

Strawberry Fair shook her beautiful mane and made twenty-four dishes of sunny strawberries and Milky Way decorated the party with an arch of shimmering stars. After the Green Gnome awarded the twenty-four magic spell books the Party Ponies hurried away.

Lollipop had remembered her key this time and as she unlocked the door to her garden they heard the nonsense gnome laughing.

''He sounds happy,'' whispered Dancing Butterflies.

''No, he laughs when he's sad,'' explained Lollipop. ''But he'll be happy to see us, then he'll cry. I told you he's a nonsense gnome.''

Sure enough the gnome started to cry when he saw the Party Ponies dashing towards him. ''That stone statue didn't come and talk to me,'' he told Lollipop.

''That's not nonsense,'' laughed Up, Up and Away. ''Signy can't walk or talk, he's got that right.''

Lollipop smiled secretly, she knew Signy could walk and talk; she was glad the statue had made friends with the nonsense gnome. ''We've come to give a special party for you,'' she said to the gnome. ''And I'd like you to stay in my garden and live in one of the lollipop-stick houses.''

''I can,'' laughed the gnome, ''I don't have to earn a living.''

''He means he *does* have to earn a living,'' sighed Love Melody.

"He can stay here and earn one!" cried Up, Up and Away. "He can make all sorts of things out of lollipop-sticks. He's really very clever."

"I wouldn't like that," replied the nonsense gnome and all the Party Ponies laughed. Then they performed their special party acts for him.

When Milky Way made a shimmering arch of stars, one of the stars landed on the gnome's hat. After that, he stopped talking nonsense. But he liked his new pony friends so much that he decided to stay in the walled garden anyway. "I wouldn't have as much fun if I went back to work for the Green Gnome," he said.

"I'll ask our Pony Land Key Maker to make you a key for the garden door," said Lollipop. "Then you can come and go whenever you like."

"I won't need one," laughed the gnome. "My name is Nod and now I don't talk nonsense, my tricks and magic spells work. I'll be able to open the door with a magic nod. And I'll never be lonely," he added, smiling at Lollipop.

Lollipop smiled back. She was glad Nod the gnome knew that Signy the stone statue could walk and talk. She knew he'd keep the secret and she was looking forward to the exciting times she knew the three of them would have together!

LOVE MELODY'S SONG BOOK I

Hello, I'm Up, Up and Away
I'll make some balloons for you today.
I'll wiggle my nose and then you'll see
Balloons a-floating so merrily.
It's party time
The fun's begun.
The magic balloon is the big red one.
Just climb on it
We're ready to go.
We'll see Pony Land friends and places I know . . .

JOURNEY ON THE MAGIC BALLOON

Amazing Acrobats

Baby Bouncy loves visiting the Amazing Acrobats.

Beautiful Bower

Dancing Butterflies likes to dance above the Beautiful Bower.

Colourful Caves

Princess Aquamarine likes to dream about the prince who lives in the Colourful Caves.

Dashing Dora

Dashing Dora, the friendly hurricane, likes to blow Tex's hat into the air so Tex can lasso it back.

Enchanted Egghouses

The Enchanted Egghouses remind Baby Quackers of the pretty pebbles she likes to collect.

Funfair Forest

The newborn twins have lots of fun when they look in the magic mirrors in Funfair Forest.

Golden Galleon

The baby sea ponies often visit the Golden Galleon to search for treasure.

Hill of Happiness

The Summer Wing ponies often collect flowers from the Hill of Happiness.

Island of Ice

When Tug hoists his magic sail his tugboat often takes him across the lake to the Island of Ice.

Jolly Juggler

Lollipop likes to teach the Jolly Juggler new tricks.

Kind Kraken

Baby Tic Tac Toe enjoys a game with Kind Kraken, the friendly sea monster.

Land of Lovehearts

Love Melody asked the magic balloon to stop for a while in the Land of Lovehearts.

Magic Mountain

Tracks never knows who he'll meet when he takes a train ride up the Magic Mountain.

Noisy Nixies

If Baby Bouncy wants to make a noise, Majesty sends her to play with the Noisy Nixies.

Orlando's Orangery

Tutti Frutti loves giving birthday parties in Orlando's Orangery.

Princess Ruby

When Princess Ruby feels restless she visits the Hair Salon for a new hair style.

Quick Queen

Quarterback often visits the Quick Queen for a game of football.

Roaring River

When the Roaring River roars, Spike's dragon friends roar back.

Secret Steps

Up, Up and Away never knows what she'll find behind the door at the top of the Secret Steps.

Twirling Turtles

The Twirling Turtles are having dancing lessons from Baby Half Note.

Umbrella Urchins

Baby Quackers often plays with the Umbrella Urchins.

Velvet Valley

Milky Way often visits Velvet Valley to dream about her next party.

Whispering Whirlpool

First Base's baseball led the way to the Whispering Whirlpool.

Xylophone

Trucker found a Xylophone in Music Land and brought it home in his truck.

Yellow Yawnies

Nurse Lollipop sometimes asks the Yellow Yawnies to send the newborn twins to sleep.

Zodiac Zone

When Baby North Star is old enough she'll visit the Zodiac Zone.

THE ENCHANTED TABLE

"Milky Way is coming to take you out," Lollipop told Fleecy and Fluffy. "Be good, won't you?"

Fleecy twitched her nose and made a noise that sounded like a violin. Fluffy drummed her tiny hooves on her rocker. "All right," laughed Milky Way, coming towards them. "You can ride around Pony Land."

"Go to Funfair Forest?" Fleecy asked hopefully. Milky Way laughed and nuzzled the newborn twin.

"Is that where you want to go, Fleecy?" asked Milky Way. "Yes please!" shouted Fleecy.

"It's a long way to Funfair Forest," said Milky Way. "We'll go and see the Key Maker first."

One of the Key Maker's keys jumped towards Fleecy's rocker. "Now, I'll wind you up," said Milky Way.

Milky Way laughed merrily as the key touched Fleecy's rocker. "Now wind Fluffy up," she ordered the key. "You'll be able to rock along the ground as quickly as I can gallop," explained Milky Way.

Before long, they arrived at Funfair Forest. "Leave your rockers here," said Milky Way. "They'll be safe."

Fleecy and Fluffy chortled loudly as the tree in front of them turned into a twirling swingaround.

The swingaround stopped and Milky Way helped the newborn twins onto a leafy seat. Before she had time to jump onto a seat, the swingaround twirled away. A woodland troll ran up to Milky Way.

"Milky Way, please help," begged the troll. "I've locked myself out of my treehouse. It's over there."

"Where will the swingaround stop?" asked Milky Way. "Don't worry, it will come back here," said the troll.

Milky Way took the key from around her neck and unlocked the door. "Thank you so much," said the troll, and he hurried inside. Milky Way turned round; the swingaround was back. But the newborn twins weren't!

Milky Way knocked on the troll's closed door. There was no reply. And the keyhole had disappeared.

"I know this key is magic," said Milky Way. "It will help me find out where Fleecy and Fluffy are!"

Meanwhile, Fleecy and Fluffy were laughing loudly as they gazed into some magic mirrors inside a tree. Suddenly, two little trolls popped out of a mirror. They had very funny faces!

"Who are you?" giggled Fluffy. "We are Quip and Quirk, the wit-snappers," said one of the funny trolls.

"We're twins, like you," said the other troll, as he pulled a whole tree from Fleecy's ear!

"You're not like us, you haven't got rockers to ride," chuckled Fleecy, peering around the funny room.

Quirk pointed to a mirror and a huge wooden table walked out of it. "We ride this," explained Quirk.

"It's an enchanted table," said Quip. "Would you like a dish of jelly?" The newborn twins loved jelly!

"Jelly!" nodded Fluffy, looking at the carved cats on the table. One of them moved a paw; a dish of jelly arrived.

"Would you like custard on your jelly?" asked Quirk, stroking the cat's ear. Fleecy laughed as a jug of custard poured itself over the jelly. "Ice-cream?" asked Fluffy. Quip pressed his nose and clapped his hands.

"You eat up while we go for a ride," Quip and Quirk told the newborn twins. Then they jumped onto the table.

The table started to walk around the room. A cat's paw held an ice-cream cornet towards Fleecy.

Quip and Quirk danced on the table and sang a song: "Eat the jelly we made for you. Yellow custard and ice-cream too. We're wit-snappers, soon you'll see just how funny we can be!"

From outside the tree, Milky Way gasped as she heard the song. The newborn twins were in danger!

The wit-snappers belonged to the Terrible Twin Wizards who liked to collect two the same of anything!

Milky Way touched one of her stars. A shimmering band of stars floated into the tree of magic mirrors.

The stars formed a cage around the newborn twins just as Milky Way arrived. "Don't eat anything!" she cried.

The enchanted table hissed angrily as Milky Way ran towards it. The cats' paws tried to claw at her. Somehow, she managed to touch the table with the magic key. Quip and Quirk shook their fists.

"Don't lick your hooves!" Milky Way begged. "If you eat anything made by Quip and Quirk their enchanted table will pick you up and carry you to the Terrible Twin Wizards." "Nice jelly," said Fluffy.

Suddenly, the enchanted table whizzed through one of the mirrors. The food followed it. The magic key had worked!

"All gone," laughed Fleecy, as the magic key went back around Milky Way's neck. "Magic!" chuckled Fluffy.

Then, the troll Milky Way had helped earlier appeared through a mirror. "I'm sorry I stopped you going on the swingaround," he said. "The wit-snappers had put a spell on all of us to make us help them."

"Some of us are twins, but we wouldn't eat their food," said another troll. "The wizards collect twin things!"

"You're safe now!" said Milky Way. "The newborn twins enjoyed themselves. They didn't know they were in danger!"

TEA PARTY IN FUNFAIR FOREST

The woodland trolls were so pleased when Milky Way sent the wit-snappers away on the enchanted table. They decided to make a special tea party for her and the newborn twins.

However, there was still some magic about, the trolls couldn't find the party food. See if *you* can find six ice-cream cornets, seven bowls of custard and a star-shaped cake.

HONE

LOVE MELODY'S SONG BOOK II

We like to rock,
We rock to and fro.
I'm Fleecy, I go high
And Fluffy goes low.
We make some strange noises
That sound like a band.
We like to ride all
Around Pony Land!

Find ten rattles hidden in this picture.

MILKY WAY AND THE WHISPERING WHIRLPOOL

Milky Way and Princess Aquamarine were great friends. They both liked to daydream and Milky Way loved listening to the princess pony's romantic stories. Prickles, Princess Aquamarine's dragon attendant, had to take even more care of Princess Aquamarine when she was with Milky Way!

Right now, everything was quiet and peaceful. Princess Aquamarine had just been to the Hair Salon. Fifi had curled and plaited her tail and mane then sprayed it with silver and gold stars. Princess Aquamarine was sitting quietly by the Silver Stream, watching her reflection.

"It's very hot, Princess Aquamarine," said Prickles. "Would you like me to make you a fan? There are some nice big ferns on the other side of the stream."

"No thank you, Prickles," replied the princess pony gently. "I don't want my curls to blow about. Fifi has arranged them so prettily."

"She has," agreed Prickles.

"They remind me of a lacy shawl."

Just then Milky Way came running towards them.

"Here's Milky Way," said Princess Aquamarine. "She's moving so fast she looks as if she's flying. Look at the sunbeams dancing over her."

"Princess Aquamarine, I've been looking everywhere for you," said Milky Way breathlessly. "Oh, you've been to the Hair Salon," she added, gazing at the princess pony's plaits and curls. "I didn't think of looking there, Prickles usually dresses your hair."

"And he does it beautifully," said Princess Aquamarine, nuzzling the little dragon. "But Princess Ruby told me about the new star spray Fifi was using and it sounded so romantic . . ."

"Of course, you had to try it," agreed Milky Way. "The stars are pretty and so are the curls."

"I think they look like a lacy shawl," Prickles told Milky Way.

"Lacy shawl! That's reminded me why I was looking for you," said Milky Way. "Last night I went up to the Whispering Whirlpool. I heard real voices, Princess Aquamarine. They whispered the same thing over and over again."

"What were they saying?" asked Prickles anxiously. He had a feeling he was going to have to guard his Princess very carefully!

"Osmunda's lacy shawl," replied Milky Way dreamily.

"Oh, no!" gasped Princess Aquamarine. "I know what that means. Listen, I'll tell you about Osmunda. She is an underwater fairy who spends all the day seadreaming. She lives in a beautiful sunken village with lots of other underwater fairies."

Milky Way sighed. "I wouldn't like to live there no matter how beautiful it is. There wouldn't be any night time stars."

"They can see the stars once every hundred years," said Princess Aquamarine. "It's then their voices can be heard on land."

"So they saw the stars last night," said Milky Way, "and I heard their voices. I wonder what they meant?"

"I'm trying to tell you," said the princess pony gently. "Every night, Osmunda has to turn her seadreams into stories. She tells the stories to Mortimer, the Sea Warrior. In return for the storytelling, Mortimer allows the underwater fairies to live in peace."

A cloud appeared over Princess Aquamarine's head and drifted gently over to Milky Way. Prickles sighed. The cloud meant that Princess Aquamarine believed her story was true. He listened carefully as she continued.

"Osmunda can't turn her seadreams into stories unless she's wearing a lacy shawl. The voices you heard, Milky Way, mean she has lost her shawl. If she can't tell Mortimer stories at night, he will cast the fairies out of their home. Then they will float to the surface of the whirlpool and disappear for ever!"

"What can we do?" whispered Milky Way. "We must help them."

"Only the one who heard the voices can help," replied Princess Aquamarine. "The only trouble is . . . any lacy shawl Osmunda wears must be under water in the sunken village."

"If only I could go safely under water I could make an arch of shimmering stars on a band of velvet," sighed Milky Way. "Osmunda could wear it as a shawl. What a lovely party we could have then." Milky Way never forgot she was one of the Party Ponies.

Just then, Princess Aquamarine's cloud started to move gently. Prickles watched carefully. Yes, the ponies were moving with it. They moved faster and faster. Poor Prickles could hardly keep up with them.

At last the ponies stopped; the cloud disappeared and Prickles hurried to Princess Aquamarine. "We're at the Hair Salon," he puffed. "Why are we here?"

"Fifi's new spray!" smiled Princess Aquamarine. "It's waterproof. Ask her to spray you all over, Milky Way. Then you'll be safe to go to Osmunda."

"Merry manes!" gasped Fifi, when Milky Way made her request. "I don't know if my spray is waterproof enough for that."

"It will have to be," said Milky Way. "I *must* try to help Osmunda. Besides," she added, "I've never given an underwater party before."

"I'll go with her to make sure she's safe," stated Princess Aquamarine. "Do as she asks, Fifi."

Fifi bobbed a dainty curtsey. The princess pony had sounded so regal! Then, carefully, she sprayed Milky Way. "You're covered in more stars now," she laughed.

Milky Way noticed how worried Prickles looked. She knew he didn't want his princess pony to go to the Whispering Whirlpool. "I'll use my unicorn magic to reach the whirlpool," she said. And the next second she had disappeared.

"Can we go and watch through Majesty's magic mirror?" begged Prickles. He wanted to see what was happening, now he knew Princess Aquamarine would be safe if Majesty was here, too.

"I'll close the Hair Salon and come with you," said Fifi. "I do hope I put enough spray on Milky Way."

"I'm sure you did," comforted Princess Aquamarine, as they hurried to Dream Castle.

"We won't be able to see what's happening under the Whispering Whirlpool," explained Majesty. "My magic mirror can only show us what's happening under water when the water is calm. But look! There's the whirlpool."

"As long as the underwater fairies don't float to the surface we'll know everything's all right," said Princess Aquamarine.

"I can see some stars!" gasped Prickles. "And it isn't night. What does that mean?"

"It might be the stars from my special spray," sighed Fifi. "Heavy hooves! Maybe it isn't waterproof enough."

Princess Aquamarine, Majesty, Fifi and Prickles gazed anxiously into the magic mirror. If only they could see under the Whispering Whirlpool! But they couldn't and every now and then stars shot out of the whirlpool.

Prickles began to cry. "We've lost Milky Way forever and ever," he sobbed.

"I shouldn't have told her the story of Osmunda and the lacy shawl," sighed Princess Aquamarine.

"You were right to tell her and Milky Way was right to try and help," Majesty spoke gently. "I'm sure Milky Way will be all right."

"She is, she is," said Fifi excitedly. "Look, I can see her, and she has still got more stars than ever. My spray *did* work."

"Let's go and meet her!" shouted Prickles. "I can't wait to hear all about her adventure."

Milky Way appeared suddenly in the throne room. She had used her unicorn magic to get home quickly. "It was the best party I've ever been to," she said dreamily. "I had to make three arches of stars before Osmunda could touch one and wear it as a shawl."

"That's why we saw all the stars shooting out," said Prickles.

"Did you hear any stories?" asked Princess Aquamarine.

"No, Osmunda can't tell them until night," explained Milky Way. "But she did give me this magic shell, and if I put it to my ear at midnight, I'll be able to hear her stories. Then I will have a special Story Party for all my friends," she added happily. "After all, I am a Party Pony!"

THE MITTEN TREE

"First Base, please let me come and play baseball tomorrow," begged Spiny. "Not tomorrow," replied First Base.

Suddenly, a loud cheer filled the air. "Quarterback has scored. Your team has won!" shouted Spiny. "I do wish I could come tomorrow," he said again. "Come the day after," said First Base. "Borrow this ball until then."

"I'm getting good at baseball," Spiny boasted, on the way home. "Did you see that catch I made, Sniffles?"

"Do it again, Spiny," laughed Sniffles. The little dragon threw the ball into the air and tried to catch it.

"Ouch! I've hurt myself!" yelled Spiny. "Come here and let me see," said Lollipop. Spiny held his paw out. "You've bruised it," sighed Lollipop. "You'll have to get some special padded mittens, Spiny."

"Lollipop will make it better," said Sniffles. "Yes, come into Lullaby Nursery, Spiny, I'll get some cream."

Afterwards, Spiny hurried home to see his friends. "I've forgotten the ball," he said. "I'll get it later."

"Would you like tea in the garden?" Lollipop asked Sniffles and Snookums. All the other newborn twins and baby ponies were out on a picnic with the Party Ponies. "Yes please," laughed Snookums.

"That pony nurse won't come outside for a while if she's making tea," muttered Get It the Goblin.

Get It worked for Wizard Wantall. He knew that his master wanted First Base's baseball. Get It chuckled.

"Hello, Sniffles and Snookums," smiled Get It. "I've just been talking to Spiny. He told me that he needed some special mittens so that he wouldn't hurt himself when he caught the baseball." Sniffles nodded.

"I'm magic," said Get It. "I know how to make a Mitten Tree grow. Would you like me to grow one for Spiny?"

"Oh, yes!" said Snookums. "First we must plant the baseball," explained Get It. "Come on."

Get It smiled to himself as he chose a place in the garden to plant the ball. He didn't really know how to make a Mitten Tree grow. He was going to come back later and dig the ball up for Wizard Wantall!

"Right, the hole's big enough," he told the newborn twins. "I'll plant the ball and cast a spell."

"Mitten Tree?" asked Snookums when the goblin had covered the ball up. "It will be there tomorrow," he said.

"Spike's baseball . . . all gone!" said Sniffles. "You can dig it up when the Mitten Tree grows," said Get It. "You mustn't tell anyone what we've done or the tree won't grow." "It's a secret," laughed Snookums.

Then Lollipop called the newborn twins for their tea. Get It climbed over the gate and hurried away.

Get It ran all the way home. He couldn't wait to tell his master how clever he'd been.

"Wizard Wantall!" cried Get It. "You know that baseball of First Base's you want? The one that can make extra baseballs? Tomorrow I will give it to you," and Get It told how he'd tricked the newborn twins.

"After midnight, when I can make myself invisible, I'll go back and dig the ball up," gloated Get It.

Meanwhile, Sniffles and Snookums had finished their tea and were looking at the place they'd planted the ball.

Spiny was on his way to fetch the baseball when two butterflies landed on his shoulders. "Hello," said Spiny. "You're Dancing Butterflies' friend aren't you?" The butterflies sang gently into Spiny's ears.

"Wizard Wantall's goblin is going to steal the baseball tonight?" repeated Spiny. "Yes," sang the butterflies.

"Roaring dragons! I'll teach him a lesson," laughed the little dragon. "Let's go and find Nod the gnome."

Spiny and the butterflies told Nod all about the trick Get It had played on Sniffles and Snookums. "The baseball can't make extra baseballs without First Base wiggling his nose," laughed Spiny. "But . . ."

"You'd like me to make a baseball with a surprise inside it?" chuckled Nod. "And some mittens," said Spiny.

"Butterflies, will you go and see if you can find Lollipop?" asked Nod. "I've got a funny idea in my head."

"I'm glad Dancing Butterflies' friends saw and heard everything that happened," said Spiny. "I can't wait to play our own trick on Get It and Wizard Wantall. Oh, good, here's Lollipop."

"The butterflies told me everything," said Lollipop. "What is your funny idea, Nod?"

"I want an extra sticky lollipop," explained Nod. "One that will fit inside this baseball shape."

"I'll put a screeching spell on the sticky lollipop," said Nod, as they all went outside to Lollipop's lollipop tree. Lollipop chose a lollipop and Nod waved his hands over it, then put it inside the baseball shape.

"We'll go and dig up the real baseball and plant this one," Nod told them. "Come on!"

Nod had picked a large plant and Lollipop helped him to tie the mittens onto it. Spiny chuckled.

"I'll stay here and keep watch," said Nod. "When Get It has dug up the ball I made, I'll re-plant your baseball, Spiny. Then I'll plant the Mitten Tree for Sniffles and Snookums to find in the morning."

Lollipop hurried into the nursery to make sure that all the ponies were still fast asleep.

"We'll go and fetch Dancing Butterflies to watch the fun," sang the butterflies and Nod nodded in agreement.

Next morning, Sniffles and Snookums hurried into the garden. "Look! Mitten Tree," laughed Snookums. "Here's Spiny," said Sniffles. "Look, Spiny, special mittens for you. Let's dig up the baseball now."

Later, as Spiny showed the newborn twins how good he was at catching the baseball, a strange screeching sound could be heard. Get It had given Wizard Wantall the trick baseball. It *did* have something extra inside!

THE RUNAWAY TOOTHPASTE

"Heavy hooves, Baby Tic Tac Toe, you'll be in trouble again!" Strawberry Fair tried not to laugh as she hurried up to the baby pony. "You know your toothpaste is for cleaning your first tooth, not for playing games with."

"Yes, but Strawberry Fair," explained Baby Tic Tac Toe earnestly, "I met a kind, old Spell Higgler. He told me all about higgling and haggling and I higgled my first tooth for a spell to rub on my tube of toothpaste!"

Strawberry Fair gasped in dismay. "You haven't given him your first tooth, have you?"

"Not yet. I've still got it, look!"

"But you just said you'd higgled your tooth for a spell," said the Party Pony. "If you've got the spell, the Spell Higgler should have your tooth."

"I've promised to let him have it when it falls out," laughed the baby pony. "First teeth do fall out you know, then another tooth grows in its place."

"I don't understand it," said Strawberry Fair. "It will be ages before you lose your first tooth."

"I told you he was a kind Spell Higgler. He said he didn't mind how long he had to wait for my tooth," explained Baby Tic Tac Toe. "Anyway, watch this, Strawberry Fair!" Baby Tic Tac Toe rubbed a small silver cloth over her tube of toothpaste. Then she took the top off and drew a Tic Tac Toe grid.

"I'll be the nought, you can be the cross," the baby pony said to the tube of toothpaste.

"All right, but I want to go first, you went first last time," squeaked the tube. Strawberry Fair laughed. The tube had a very funny voice. "Be quiet, Strawberry Fair!" commanded the tube. "I have to think very hard when I play this game."

"Sorry," muttered the pony, and sat down quietly to watch. Even though the tube of toothpaste seemed to think very hard before it put its crosses in the squares, Baby Tic Tac Toe won three games in a row.

"That's enough," she said. "We'll play again later." She waved the small silver cloth over all the toothpaste games and the toothpaste put itself back into the tube!

"There," she said, smiling at Strawberry Fair. "I won't be in trouble for playing with my toothpaste because I'm not wasting it."

Just then, Strawberry Fair and Baby Tic Tac Toe heard the sound of a train coming nearer and nearer. "Tracks has made his model train full-size!" shouted Baby Tic Tac Toe. "Happy hooves! I do hope he'll stop and give us a ride."

"All aboard for adventure!" called Tracks, bringing the train to a halt. "Climb up, Strawberry Fair, you can sit next to me."

"Thank you, Tracks," laughed Strawberry Fair, as she climbed in beside the Adventure Boy pony. "I hope you're not taking us on a long journey. I said I'd meet Dancing Butterflies by the Waterfall at four o'clock."

"We won't be going far," replied Tracks. "I want to go and tell Majesty about a strange Spell Higgler who got on my train. Do you know, he tried to make me higgle my train for one of his spells! I didn't trust him at all. I'm sure he was up to no good. I made him get off my train."

"Baby Tic Tac Toe higgled a spell with him," gasped Strawberry Fair. "Tell him about it . . ." But the baby pony wasn't there.

"She must have climbed into one of the carriages," said Tracks. He stopped the train again and jumped out. "Where are you, Baby Tic Tac Toe?" he called loudly. There was no reply.

"I'm sure I saw her climbing up behind me," said Strawberry Fair, who had followed Tracks. "She was really excited when we heard the train. She wanted a ride, she said so."

"We've not come very far," said Tracks. "She must be somewhere around."

Suddenly, Strawberry Fair heard someone crying. "That sounds like Baby Tic Tac Toe," she said. "But where is she? I still can't see her."

"The crying is coming from behind that hedge," decided Tracks. "Come on, we'll soon see what's wrong." Tracks was right; as they hurried towards the hedge the crying became louder.

But it wasn't Baby Tic Tac Toe. It was Baby Bouncy! "Oh, Strawberry Fair," sobbed the baby pony, as the pony stopped in front of her, "my space-hopper ball bounced away all by itself. I found this little silver cloth and I used it to clean a mark off my space-hopper . . . then . . . it just bounced away!"

"That's the spell Baby Tic Tac Toe higgled with the Spell Higgler," Strawberry Fair told Tracks, pointing to the silver cloth.

"I saw Baby Tic Tac Toe galloping very fast that way," said Baby Bouncy. "I was going to follow her then I noticed the mark on my space-hopper and I saw the silver cloth and I . . ."

"All right, we know what happened next," said Strawberry Fair, nuzzling Baby Bouncy. Then she looked up at Tracks. "I think Baby Tic Tac Toe rubbed her tube of toothpaste with the silver cloth," she stated.

"Yes," agreed Tracks. "Then the tube of toothpaste ran away and she followed it. Somebody somewhere wants a baby pony. But who and why, and how can we find out where?"

"I know!" cried Strawberry Fair. "Let's rub the silver cloth all over your train, then *it* might run away to the same place. We'll get on the train and rub the cloth over the inside."

"Magnificent manes!" said Tracks. "That's a marvellous idea, we won't have to follow the train, we'll be on it."

"I'm coming with you," said Baby Bouncy, bouncing up quickly. "I'll be good and do exactly what I'm told," she added, looking up at the big Adventure Boy pony.

"All right," said Tracks. "All aboard for adventure!"

Strawberry Fair hadn't rubbed much of the train with the silver cloth before it started to move very fast indeed. "It's never moved this quickly before!" shouted Tracks.

"I'm frightened, I want to get off, I'm going to fly," gabbled Baby Bouncy.

"No, you must stay with us," Tracks told her. "I'll look after you, don't worry, Baby Bouncy." The baby pony snuggled up to him and although Tracks had told her not to worry, he felt very worried himself!

Strawberry Fair peered out of the

train but it was moving so quickly everything was a blur. She couldn't see where they were at all. "Everything looks pink and white and yellow," she said. "And . . ."

"We're slowing down," said Tracks. "We've stopped. Let's get out and see where we are. You stay close to me, Baby Bouncy." So the three of them climbed down from the train.

"We're walking in toothpaste," giggled Baby Bouncy, forgetting all about being frightened. "Oh, it does taste nice," she added, nibbling some from her hoof. "It tastes of all the strawberry sundaes that Strawberry Fair makes best."

"Here comes that Spell Higgler," Tracks spoke grimly. "Now we'll see what all this is about."

"Baby Tic Tac Toe is with him!" shouted Strawberry Fair, as the Spell Higgler waded through the deep toothpaste towards them.

"I'm so glad you've come," gasped the Spell Higgler. "Please help me. My toothpaste wand is buried somewhere under all this toothpaste. Until I find it, the toothpaste will just keep spreading and growing. Before long the whole of my land will be covered in toothpaste . . ."

"Why didn't you just tell us what was wrong?" demanded Tracks. "Why did you try and higgle spells with us?"

"You have to higgle and haggle for things," said the Spell Higgler, sounding surprised. "If I'd just asked you to come you wouldn't have come for nothing in exchange. Besides, you wouldn't have

believed me if I'd told you about all this toothpaste. You'd have thought it was a trick. I had to use higgle-haggle to get you here."

"You are silly," laughed Strawberry Fair. "Of course we'd have helped you without any higgle-haggle. Never mind, we're here now. What can we do?"

"I'm not sure," admitted the Spell Higgler. "I only know that somehow I've got to find my wand. Then I can stop all this toothpaste from spreading and growing. Look at it now, it's getting deeper."

"What would happen if I rubbed the toothpaste with the silver cloth you higgled with Baby Tic Tac Toe?" asked Strawberry Fair.

"The spell inside the silver cloth made the tube of toothpaste, the space-hopper and the train come here," said Tracks thoughtfully. "Can't you make some more silver cloths with spells in?" he asked the Spell Higgler. "Spells that would make all this toothpaste run onto my train."

"Then we could find your wand," said Baby Bouncy, bouncing happily through the toothpaste.

Before long, they were all rubbing at the toothpaste with silver cloths. The baby ponies screamed and laughed as the toothpaste streamed onto the train. And at last the Spell Higgler found his wand.

He muttered some strange words, waved the wand and the toothpaste disappeared out of the train.

"Where has it gone?" asked Baby Tic Tac Toe. "I've still got my tube of toothpaste."

"I don't know where it's gone," said the Spell Higgler. "It doesn't matter though. Whenever I need to make toothpaste to put into tubes, for first tooth ponies, I'll wave my wand and it will be there. Only I'll make sure I never let my wand get buried again."

"I hope you'll remember you

don't have to higgle-haggle for everything," Strawberry Fair said sternly.

"I like higgling!" said Baby Tic Tac Toe. "I higgled my first tooth for a spell."

"We'll unhiggle the higgle," twinkled the Spell Higgler. "You give me the silver cloth back and you can keep your first tooth. Don't worry," he added, "your tube of toothpaste will always be magic, Baby Tic Tac Toe. But it will never take you anywhere unless you ask it to."

"Ask it to take us back to Pony Land," suggested Strawberry Fair.

"I don't want to go without my space-hopper," said Baby Bouncy.

"It's already on the train," the Spell Higgler told her. "I do hope you'll come and visit me again," he said, as Tracks climbed onto the train.

"We will," promised Tracks. "All aboard for adventure."

"Tube of toothpaste, take us to Pony Land," chuckled Baby Tic Tac Toe.

"Oh, look," said Baby Bouncy, as the train sped away, "there are lots of tubes of toothpaste tied to my space-hopper. I wonder if they're magic, too?"

"You'll just have to wait and see," said Tracks, as the train stopped at the Waterfall, where Dancing Butterflies was waiting for Strawberry Fair.

"All the toothpaste will taste of your favourite party fruits," laughed Strawberry Fair, as she trotted away with Dancing Butterflies. "And maybe they'll be magic too . . ."

MIDNIGHT MAGIC

It was the morning of New Year's Eve and the Magic Message Ponies were very excited. They'd never been in Pony Land on New Year's Eve before.

"I'm going to practise flying my kite all day," said Magical Breeze. "I want to be sure I can make it fly very high at midnight, to welcome in the New Year!"

"There isn't much wind today," sighed Floater. "I wanted to go for a balloon ride."

"I'll soon put that right," laughed Magical Breeze. "Go and get your basket, Floater."

"I'm going on a very long journey," Floater told her friends, as she tied some balloons onto her basket. "I'm going to the Land of Balloons. I want to bring some special balloons back to celebrate the New Year."

"Can I come with you?" Cloud Dreamer asked eagerly. "I love being close to the clouds."

"Happy hooves, of course you can! It's much more fun when I have a passenger," replied Floater. "There, the basket is ready. Let's climb in, Cloud Dreamer, and wait for Magical Breeze to make it windy."

Magical Breeze had her own special tree that could call up a wind whenever it was needed.

Floater and Cloud Dreamer laughed excitedly as Magical Breeze gently swished her tail.

"We want windy weather for kite flying and balloon riding," whispered Magical Breeze. She smiled as her kite appeared, then waved to Floater and Cloud Dreamer as the wind lifted the basket into the sky.

Before long, Magical Breeze's kite was flying high in the sky. "I'm getting much better," she said to herself. "I didn't get the string tangled in anything this time."

"I was hoping the string would get caught in my branches," said a nearby tree.

Magical Breeze giggled. "Then you'd have to untangle the string for me and I'd give you some apples as a reward," she said. "I tell you what. I'll give you some apples anyway." She wiggled her nose and a dozen red apples appeared on the branches of the tree.

"Thank you," said the tree. "I'll be sure to help you next time you get your kite caught in my branches."

"I wish you could help me," said Magic Hat, appearing from behind the tree. "I waved my wand over my hat and a rabbit jumped out. But he ran away and I can't find him anywhere."

"I can't find him either," said a

little bird, as he flew down to Magic Hat. "You must have waved your wand too quickly."

"I'll just bring my kite down then I'll help you look for the rabbit," said Magical Breeze. "Maybe he's playing with Teddi's teddy bear or looking at pictures in Mirror Mirror's magic mirror."

"No, he isn't," sighed Magic Hat. "Mirror Mirror is cleaning her magic mirror, ready for tonight, and Teddi is mending a teddy bear for a baby pixie. My rabbit isn't with them. I just don't know where he can be."

Floater and Cloud Dreamer knew where Magic Hat's rabbit was. He was in the balloon basket with them. He had jumped in when nobody was looking and he'd given the two ponies quite a fright when he'd suddenly popped up from the bottom of the basket!

"You'll have to come with us," said Floater. "I'm not turning back now."

"Happy ears!" said the rabbit cheekily. "I don't want you to. This is much more fun than jumping in and out of Magic Hat's hat!"

"Magic Hat will be worried about you," scolded Cloud Dreamer.

"She'll be all right," said the cheeky rabbit. "She can play with her other friend, Billy the bird. Oh, look, Cloud Dreamer! That cloud is turning into a white castle."

"Floater, can we stay here for a while and go inside the castle?" asked Cloud Dreamer.

"Only for a little while," said Floater. "We've still got a long way to go to the Land of Balloons."

"Look!Look!" shouted the rabbit, jumping out of the basket. "There's a little white dragon in one of the towers. Let's go and visit him."

Cloud Dreamer smiled happily. She knew all about the little white dragon. He was her own magic friend!

"I wish I could stay here all day," said the rabbit. "I love this castle with its silvery, sparkling walls."

"Shall we leave the rabbit here and collect him on the way back from the Land of Balloons?" Floater suggested to Cloud Dreamer.

"That's a good idea," replied Cloud Dreamer. "Rabbit's a bit cheeky, he might upset the folk in the Land of Balloons. He won't upset the little white dragon; he can be cheeky, too."

So Floater and Cloud Dreamer climbed back into the balloon basket. "I'm hungry," said Cloud Dreamer, as the basket moved off.

"Choose a cloud and I'll turn it into an ice-cream," laughed Floater.

"That one!" said Cloud Dreamer. "It looks like an ice-cream cone." Floater whispered some magic words

and the next second both ponies where happily munching a chocolate cornet!

After a while, the ponies arrived at the Land of Balloons. Everyone was very happy to see Floater. They knew she'd leave them lots of ice-cream cornets in exchange for the special balloons she'd come to collect.

And while Floater packed the balloons into the basket, Cloud Dreamer made pictures in the clouds for the balloon folk to look at. ''We'll have to go now,'' said Floater, as the pictures turned back into an ordinary cloud again. ''Thank you for the balloons, we'll blow them up at midnight, when we welcome in the New Year.''

''Thank you for the cloud pictures, Cloud Dreamer,'' said the balloon folk. ''And thank you, Floater, for the ice-creams,'' they added, as Floater turned a pretty cloud into chocolate cornets.

''We'll have to hurry,'' Floater said to Cloud Dreamer. ''It's getting late. I do hope we can remember the way to your cloud castle.''

"Merry manes, that's no problem," laughed Cloud Dreamer. ''My unicorn magic lets me find the castle in the cloud anytime I like."

''I hope we can find the cheeky rabbit,'' said Floater. ''He belongs to Magic Hat and only her magic will find him if he disappears.''

''Yes, and sometimes her magic takes ages and ages to work,'' agreed Cloud Dreamer. "But look, it's all right. Rabbit is waiting on that sunbeam over there."

Rabbit hopped into the balloon basket and by the time it landed, he was fast asleep. "We'll leave him there and tell Magic Hat to come and fetch him," decided Floater. "I think I'll leave the balloons here, too. We can fetch them just before midnight. Oh, I can hardly wait until it's time to blow them up."

"I'm going for a sleep," yawned Cloud Dreamer. "It was a lovely ride, Floater. I'll see you later."

The first stroke of midnight was ringing out over Pony Land. Floater had given all the little ponies, and their friends, a balloon to blow up. "You must finish blowing them up by the last stroke of midnight," she told everyone.

Magical Breeze had tied her kite to the branches of her friendly tree. "You'll have to fly my kite for me," she said. "I can't blow up a balloon and fly my kite at the same time."

On the last stroke of midnight all the balloons floated into the starry sky. They turned into one enormous balloon. And on it was a magic message from Floater to everyone in Pony Land and all their friends! "And a Happy New Year, too!" added Floater.

A RACE TO THE HAIR SALON

You need

one button or counter for each player and a dice

How to Play

1. Throw the dice and move your counter forward the same number of places as the number on the dice.
2. If you land on a picture place, look at the key to see what you have to do.
3. The winner is the first player to reach the Hair Salon.

Key

ribbon: go forward two spaces

brush: go back two spaces

roller: miss a throw

shampoo: have another throw

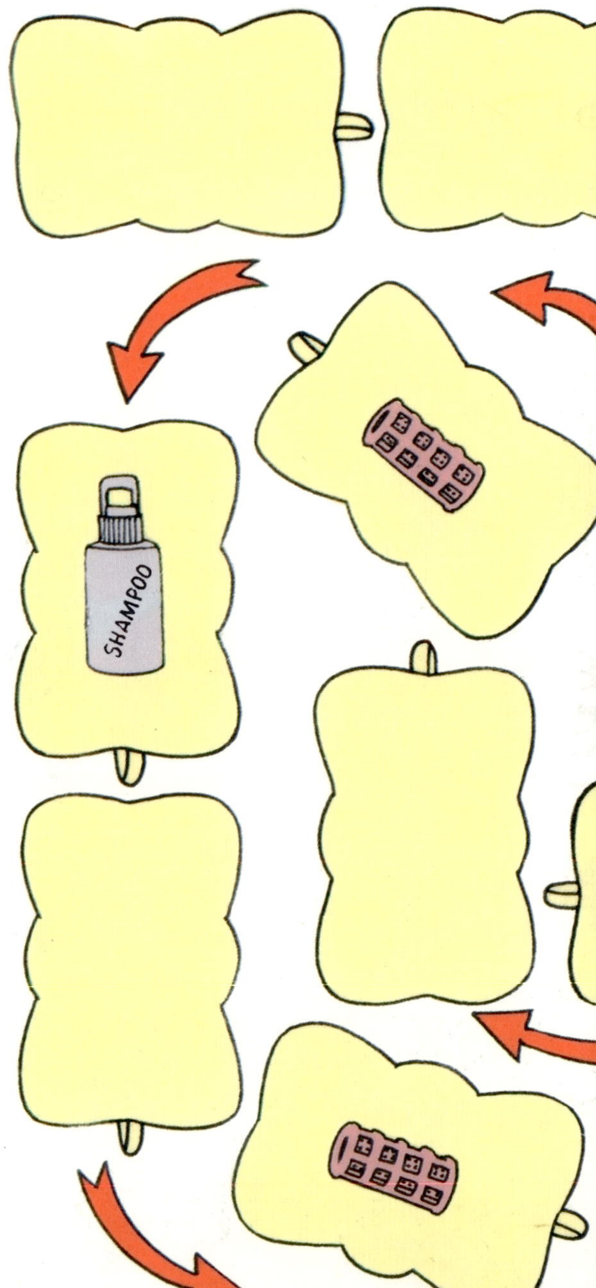